&Superstox Stock Cars

The Golden Years

&Superstox Stock Cars

The Golden Years

Richard John Neil

TEMPUS

First published 2005

Tempus Publishing Limited
The Mill, Brimscombe Port,
Stroud, Gloucestershire, GL5 2QG
www.tempus-publishing.com

British Library Cataloguing in Publication Data.
A catalogue record for this book is available from the British Library.

ISBN 0 7524 3609 0

Typesetting and origination by Tempus Publishing Limited.
Printed in Great Britain.

Contents

Acknowledgements

My very grateful thanks go to the following for their help with this book: David Band, Glenn Burtenshaw, Fred Buss, Robin Clarke, Dominic Dalton, Judy & Gerry Hall, Sonny & Barbara Howard, Frank Love, Mac McCormack, Graeme Mearns (GM Photos), Steve Monk, the Eric Setchell Collection, Mark Tegardine, Andy Weltch, Dave and Rita Willis. Sources include the *Spedeworth Spedeweek* magazine and the book *Living With Spede*. Thanks also to my lovely wife Michele (for everything) and also Mum and Dad for giving me the hobby in the first place.

Introduction

Stock Car racing came to the UK in 1954 with the first meeting taking place at New Cross in South London. The original cars were just that – 'stock', some even being driven to the circuit. As the years progressed drivers developed the cars to gain more performance and this led to some serious modifications that ultimately made the cars look less and less like the original vehicles.

Racing for original 'stock' models was catered for by occasional Banger races. These proved successful and so, in 1968, the Spedeworth promotion introduced a new formula that would be based on the original car rather than a specially built chassis. The disadvantage of Banger racing was that cars generally only lasted for one meeting and so the new formula would allow bumpers front and rear to protect the car from damage and, perhaps more importantly, to assist in the removal of slower drivers!

With the addition of the new formula, this was probably the point that 'Stock Car racing' became the generic term for all the classes that were racing on the small oval circuits. Hot rods provided the non-contact saloon car racing while the evolved, modified cars became known as Superstox. The new class was called Stock Saloon Cars and it was very quickly providing full grids with entertaining races.

Both classes grew in other countries as well. The Superstox continued to contest genuine international events with entrants from across mainland Europe and South Africa. The stock cars took off immediately (sometimes literally) in Scotland and later developed in Europe as well, although the left-hand drive Europeans never fared too well over here.

Banger meetings continued as well but the racing also tended to reflect the fact that the cars were disposable. Stock Car racing as a sport in its own right was really somewhere between outright trashing of cars and pure non-contact competition. The art of fast racing while using the front bumper to nudge or spin an opponent out of the way was something very unique that needed as much discipline as non-contact events. As well as using the front bumper, a decent driver would be able to cope with attacks on his or her rear bumper too. That's what the racing was all about. Speed, winning races, removing the opposition and staying put – if you could. Finally you need to consider that the best drivers had to fight their way through grids of up to forty cars. Superstox and stock cars provided some all-out action down the years but there was always a little more to it than met the eye.

Naturally both the Superstox and Stock Car formulae continued to evolve over the years. These days the superstox are purpose-built specials that look nothing like the cars raced in the late 1960s and early 1970s. Stock cars do still resemble present-day road cars although the machinery underneath had become more and more specialised, so a 'back-to-basics' 1,300cc version was introduced several seasons ago to get back to the spirit of the original formula.

As I mentioned in my other oval racing volume, *Hot Rod Racing – The Golden Years*, there is really no start or finishing point to the 'golden era', so this book can only provide a small glimpse at some of the key players from some happy times.

Richard John Neil, June 2005

one

Stock Cars

432

Three of the biggest names in early Stock Car racing pictured at Wimbledon in 1969. It's Dave Willis's MG Magnette. From left to right are Graham North, Foxy Dance and Dave 'Blondie' Willis.

Opposite, above: Probably better known as a Hot Rod driver and constructor, Sonny Howard started his short oval career in Stock Saloons with this MG Magnette. He later moved into Superstox and then finally into hot rods.

Opposite, below: Cross in Hand in Sussex was originally a dirt track but was revamped into a concrete raceway for the 1969 season. The circuit was only to remain open until 1972 when local residents managed to close it down. Here, though, we see it immaculate and ready for the first meeting with the new surface.

The Cross in Hand Stock Cars aftermath! Dave Willis (665) and Chris Gautrey (184) are parked up close. Gautrey won the 1971 British Championship and also went on to be a top Hot Rod driver. Also on the centre green here are Graham North (267) and Ted Simmons (297 – just behind the 184 fin plate).

Early seventies action at Wimbledon Stadium with a variety of models in shot – an MG Magnette, Ford Cortina and even a Ford Popular.

Above: John Porter (192) and Peter Thorp (272) at high speed under the lights at Wimbledon in 1971.

Opposite, below: Kent racer Brian Edwards on the grand parade at Cross in Hand raceway in 1969. Superstox (on the back straight) are sharing the bill at this meeting.

A good Sunday afternoon crowd anticipates the rolling start of another frenetic Stock Car race at Cross in Hand.

Scottish Stock Car stars John Davidson and Kenny Ireland. John was a top saloon man in the 1970s. Kenny Ireland won the Scottish Championship in each of the three formulas racing north of the border (Superstox, Stock Cars and Hot Rods).

Opposite, below: Marty Page (594) bounces off onto the Ipswich centre green while blue-top Chas Willsher (712) powers past in his Magnette. Page is a popular driver who has tried most formulae over the years, all with a certain amount of success.

Kenny Ireland (196) and Howie Jarman (40). Howie was the father of future star driver Keith and a good driver in his own right, having finished fourth in the 1971 Scottish Points Championship. This picture was taken in 1972, Kenny's last season in Stock Saloons before a single year in Superstox.

Alan Burtenshaw's Ford Consul Capri in action at Aldershot Stadium in 1973. An unusual stock car, it started as a road car taken in part exchange at a Ford dealership where Alan worked: 'Although it was halfway through the season we decided to build the car straight away. In less than a month we had stripped it down to bare essentials, put in a roll cage and ironed the car up with lengths of two-inch box iron that we bought from Dave Willis in the pits one Wednesday night at Arlington. The 1,500cc engine came out and was stripped and rebuilt by Southern Engine Services.'

Opposite, above: Mick 'Duffy' Collard took time off racing hot rods to compete with this MG Magnette in the Stock Cars during 1973. This shot was taken at the British Championship meeting at Wisbech.

Opposite, below: The first ever Stock Car European Champion Gray Davis in action at Ipswich. He won the European title in 1973. He also led the points championship in 1971 for a short while and was twice British Champion, first in 1970 and then again two years later. Gray was one of the first star drivers from the Stock Cars to switch to Hot Rods. He later moved into long-circuit racing, specialising in MGs. Gray is dicing here with Barry 'Twiggy' Cousins (667) and David Sey (627).

Spedeworth Scotland action at Cowdenbeath. Andy Johnston (195) disposes of Davy Philp (299) in 1973. This was Davy's last season in contact racing as he moved into hot rods in 1974 and later onto the long circuits.

1973 red top Derek Smith pulls off a double disposal by spinning an unidentified red-graded driver along with yellow-graded Malcolm Lane (483).

Legendary Scottish racer Robert Bruce with what was very possibly his first ever wreck at Cowdenbeath in 1973.

Long-time racer Alan 'Noddy' Robinson (432) spinning the similar Magnette of blue top Hal Danby (22). Robinson went on to become World Champion in Stock Cars by winning the 1985 title at Ruisbrook in Belgium.

Ladies' night was an annual fixture on the Spedeworth raceways. This one took place in July 1974 at Aldershot. This is Barrie Dalton's wife, Angela, on the grand parade. During the course of the meeting the driver's seat sheered off and had to be tied in with rope for the remainder of the meeting!

Opposite, above: On the face of it this photo shows Abb King (812) and Barrie Dalton (85) racing at Aldershot. In actual fact it's from the ladies' racing and features Carole King and Angela Dalton.

Opposite, below: 1973 was a strange season for Stock Cars as the traditional roof colour grading was done away with in favour of two groups, 'A' and 'B', the latter being the 'star' drivers. This picture shows a group 'A' line up at Ipswich: Charlie Brown (644 – 1973 British Champion), Pedler Palmer (90), Ron Smith (708), Malcolm Lane (483), John Kiddell (132) and Pete Hardy (236). The traditional roof colour gradings were back in place by the end of the season.

Lindsay Horstead (129) racing against Bob Studd (499) at Wisbech. Bob Studd was the first East Anglian star in the formula – he won the National Points Championship in 1971.

Roll-over weeks occurred long before the advent of the National Lottery. This one happened at Cowdenbeath in Scotland on 13 May 1973. The driver in question is Jack Robertson from Port Seton.

Superstox and stock cars take to the Yarmouth circuit for a grand parade in 1974. The stock car field shows that the fashion was a mix of MG Magnettes, Ford Cortinas, long hair and sideburns!

Paul Tegardine has the choice of two cars here. Cortinas were first made popular in Scotland and would have probably been the preferable to the brand-new Alfa Romeo.

Peter Sheen (414) was a well-known, successful and colourful driver on the Southern circuits in the early to mid-1970s. Peter is seen here in the company of Roland Usher (87) and Brian Smith (374).

Opposite, above: Two fast and popular East Anglian drivers in action. The late Paul Tegardine's Cortina (163) chases Conrad Self's Zodiac (636) with Peter Smith's Cortina on the outside line. Paul also followed Conrad across the line in the 1976 British Championship as the Anglians took second and third behind Graham Kircher. Tegardine also took the runner-up slot in the English Championship that year – also at Wimbledon.

Opposite, below: Barrie Dalton (85) gets stuck in at Matcham's Park, Ringwood in April 1975. The recipient is Tony Mitchell (203) from Winchester.

Caterham-based white-top driver Dave Cliff pictured in the pits at Wimbledon in 1975. Behind Dave's car is fellow white-grader Brian Neave (372).

Jeff Munn on the back straight in a grand parade at Arlington, Monday 26 May 1975. Jeff was one of the formula's first real superstars and was points champion in 1972, 1974 and 1975 (there was no points chart for the class in 1973). He also won the British Championship in 1974 and the European Championship held at Kaldenkirchen in Germany in 1975.

Phil Roberts and his MG Magnette (396) on the grand parade at Arlington Stadium. The Stock Cars are sharing the bill with a rookie-only Hot Rod meeting.

Dust up at the 1975 Ipswich Spede Weekend. Londoner Gerry Davies (296) is the main subject here, taking some evasive action on the inner speedway circuit. Immediately in front of Gerry is A60, Ray Molyneux. The other cars in shot are Tony Jones (776), Sam Eglin (438) and the nose of Geoff Stow's Magnette.

Keith Jarman (46) and 'Diesel' Jock Robertson (235) get well acquainted at Cowdenbeath in 1975.

Dave Davenport's 1975 mount, a Fiat 1800, in the mix with Southern-based white-top John Murray (678). Peter Smith (299) will no doubt take advantage of the clear line on the outside.

Colchester yellow-graded driver Barry Cousins (667) comes to rest after a spin at Ipswich. Peter Sheen (414) is kicking up the dust in the background.

Aubrey 'Foxy' Dance was the Stock Cars National Points Champion in the formula's second and third seasons (1969 and 1970). This shot was taken in 1975 one year before his move into hot rods.

Red-grade Conrad Self (636) has caught and passed the blue-graded duo of Horry Barnes (562) and Tony Jones (776). Rooftop mascots are in evidence here. Self's car sports a Rolls Royce flying lady while Barnes's has a pink elephant.

Peter 'Dinky' Dalton climbs out of his car after a retirement at Ipswich in 1976. Dalton never had much luck in the major championships but was a consistent driver who stayed in the top grade for several seasons.

Jack Dain (931) tries to take out Norwich racer Stu Piper (340). Both drivers went on to attain star grade in the Stock Cars later in their careers. Piper's choice of car may have had some bearing on his success – the Triumph was to become one of the formula's 'cars to have' later in the 1970s.

Yellow-top Geoff Hubbard (274) spins his big Ford Zodiac out of contention as Horry Barnes powers past on the outside line.

Scottish heroes Robert Bruce (330) and Keith Jarman (46 – racing his first ever stock saloon) get stuck in to some typical north-of-the-border action at Cowdenbeath.

The then-reigning British Champion Terry Thorp cuts inside Steve Rapley's MG Magnette (493) at Ipswich at the 1976 Spedeweekend.

East Anglian star Dave Davenport (130) seen here dicing with Sussex-based Derek Keeley (105) at Ipswich in 1976. Dave held the silver roof (denoting the national points leader) for a short while in his career.

Brian Sayers (402) and Tex Tilby (8) take their battle onto the inner Speedway track at Ipswich. Both men were top drivers on the Southern Stock Saloon scene in the mid to late seventies.

Horry Barnes leads Tony Jones and yellow-graded Ray Goudy. Just leading this pack is the rear end of Sussex star Graham Kircher.

Opposite, above: Ricky Royle looks to rejoin the circuit at Ipswich after a spin. Brian Sayers (402) motors past with Jack Dain (931) chasing.

Opposite, below: Jeff Olding was National Points leader at the time of this picture, the 1976 Spedeweekend. The car has a very distinctive set-up with the rear end jacked up considerably more than many of the other cars at the time.

White-top Robert Wolf (45) being spun by yellow-top Graham Nunn (265) at Ipswich.

A stock car line up under the flags at Ipswich. From left to right: John Wren (number not in view), Ricky Royle (459), Dick Hall (558), Tony Jones (776), Ray Molyneux (733), Gerry Davies (296), Steve Rapley (493), Peter Smith (299) and Pete Barrett (447).

Peter Dalton (275) gets spun by Southern star driver Geoff Morris (591) at Ipswich in 1976. Tex Tilby passes on the outside line.

Jeff Olding may have been leading the points championship in July 1976 but he was out of luck in this race at Ipswich. This shot affords a good view of the sort of metalwork that was used to remove the opposition.

Contact! Yellow-top Geoff Hubbard (274) gets collected after white-top Robert Wolf's (45) spin at Ipswich.

Close action on the back straight at Foxhall. Ipswich-based white-top Nigel Trench (525) leans on Wisbech's Graham Nunn (265). Check out the angle of the metal fence post just to the right of Nunn's front bumper – evidence of some hard crashes from the stock cars.

Dave Davenport (130) leads Wally Hall (99) with Dick Doddington (272) almost eclipsed on the outside line. Hall was one of the biggest characters of the formula and an able driver who was runner-up in the 1978 English Championship at Wimbledon.

The classic Stock Car rivalry pictured here – East Anglia v. the South East. Anglian man Willie Barnes (126) leads Steve Rapley (493).

1975 East Anglian Champion Tony Jones (776) heading into the third-turn bend at Ipswich.

Plenty going on here! Geoff Morris (shown head-on here) in the thick of things at Ipswich. It looks like he's dealt with yellow-top Alan Pye (512) as Terry Thorp (137) and Colin Cole (703) go past.

Three wide on the back straight! Kenny Cooke (923) dicing with Peter Smith (299) and Eddie Aldous (238). Aldous's Magnette is sporting the cross of St George on its roof, indicating that he was the reigning English champion.

Peter 'Pedro' Smith (299) switched from MG Magnette to Ford Cortina in 1976. Here he dives up the inside of John Wren (811).

Two different types of Magnette. John Wren (811) is driving a ZB while Ray Goudy's is the ZA (156). Goudy, pictured here as a yellow-top early in his career, went on to be a multi-title winner with honours including the 1979 English and 1985 European Championships.

The legendary Horry Barnes in action at Ipswich in 1976 – a mere twenty-three years into his career. Horry's racing days go back well over fifty years – he celebrated his fiftieth year in the sport in a special meeting at King's Lynn in November 2003.

Terry Thorp dons his helmet prior to a 1976 race at Ipswich. Lining up next to Terry is Jeff Olding, who is the subject of a pre-race check by one of the track staff.

Crawley in West Sussex was home to a large number of drivers including Joe Morbelli, who was also a regular Banger driver. Graham North (267) is in the background here in the Wimbledon pit area.

Blue grade line up for the 1978 National Championship at Ipswich. The main subject of this shot is Norwich driver Chris Culley (642). The tail end of Robert George's Cortina can just be seen edging into the left-hand side of the shot. Other drivers shown are Tex Tilby (8), Fred Blunsom (268), Brian Cox (297) and Alan Pye (512).

A packed stand at the 1978 Spedeweekend watches Dave Olding collect his trophy for winning the 1978 National Stock Car Championship. It had been a tough race with Olding having been given a run for his money by Scottish aces Robert Bruce and Keith Jarman. Right of shot on the podium is Spedeworth's racing manager John Clark, who also commentated at this race.

Dereham-based star-grade driver Mick Juby came to grief in the 1978 Stock Car National Championship at Ipswich and needs a tow back to the pit area.

Stock Car star Chris Olding arrives at Wimbledon stadium in September 1978.

In English domestic racing the rivalry was usually between the Southern and East Anglian drivers. Internationals were a different matter, however, with the home drivers always keen to 'sort out' the serious competition from the visitors. Eddie George (226) is the visitor here at Cowdenbeath in 1978 and is clearly regarded as a big threat (the chequered roof shows he was the reigning British Champion) but the locals have pretty well wiped him out!

Ford Escorts were really becoming the cars to have in Stock Cars. Mick Sandom was a regular star driver and is pictured here in 1979 in the Arlington pit area. The 505 car sports the famous red-and-yellow colours of the Yateley Commercial team that was predominantly seen on Bangers and Super Rods.

Northern Ireland's equivalent of Stock Cars and Superstox. The late Davy Evans (Chevette, 32) was a star driver in Super Saloons, a light-contact formula, before moving into hot rods while Ian McKnight (eventually the 1992 Superstox World Champion) was the man to beat in the Formula Two Stock Cars. The pair are pictured in the pit area at Aghadowey in August 1979.

Like Davy Evans, Norman Woolsey was another future Hot Rod World Champion who graduated from the Northern Ireland Super Saloon formula.

Alan McHattie comes to grief in 1979. Alan was originally a Saloon driver with Spedeworth Scotland but moved to Gordon McDougal Promotions in time for their opener at Newtongrange in 1981. He stayed with the saloons with GMP until the mid-1980s when he moved to hot rods and became one of GMP's top drivers. When Newtongrange shut its doors at the start of the 1989 season, Alan departed from the sport.

Steve Templeman wipes his eyes while racing an unusual Fiat stock car at a wet Arlington meeting in 1979. Left-hand drive means that the driver is on the side of the car that is most likely to hit the fence and those steel girder posts don't look too inviting. Nowadays Arlington is lined with a concrete wall. Steve made it to blue grade in this car.

two

Superstox

Like most tracks in the late 1960s and early 1970s, Lydden ciruit in Kent attracted huge crowds. Although normally a road course or Rallycross venue Lydden affords fans great views of the circuit right the way from Chessons (far left in the picture) through to Devils Elbow (just out of shot on the right).

Stock Car racing has always been a family sport, both for competitors and spectators. Sussex Superstox racer Pete Tombs (102) poses with his family *c.* 1968. Pete raced on into the 1970s with outings in Bangers.

1968 action at Cowdenbeath Stadium in Scotland. Bill Pullar (81) tangles with another car. Thomas Cairns (76) is parked up just behind Pullar.

Some things never change… Johnnie Walker remains one of the country's best and most popular radio presenters more than thirty-five years on from when this picture was taken. These days, however, he's on Radio Two rather than Radio One. He no longer races superstox although I've no doubt he'd be made very welcome at a race meeting.

Biffo Sweeney emerges from the tunnel at Wimbledon on the grand parade.

The Cayzer family from Saffron Walden were prominent racers throughout the 1970s (and indeed the next generation are still racing today). Most race fans will remember the father and sons team, Ron, John and Alan, but a fourth member of the family, Peter (cousin to John and Alan), also raced for a short while in the early 1970s.

The trackside marshals are often taken for granted in short-track racing but they have an important role to play in the proceedings. Here they are all a blur as they swiftly open the Wimbledon pit gate after a Superstox race.

More work for the marshals as two superstox tangle on Wimbledon's pit bend. Yellow flags instruct the drivers on circuit to use caution as the race continues.

The immaculate cars of the South African team line up for the 1970 World Championship at Wimbledon. From left to right are Anne Kroeze, Piet De Klerk, Fritz De Klerk and Koos Maree.

The first ever Italian entrant in the Superstox World Championship was Bernardo Balboni, who borrowed a car for the 1970 race. The affiliation with the Italian promoter never really blossomed although a further two drivers made the journey to Wimbledon for the following year's race as well.

Some of the weird and wonderful European runners from 1970 World Superstox Championship. Dutchman Piet Kleyngeld is nearest the camera. His rear-engine car finished the race in the fence.

Several of England's top drivers await the grid draw for the 1970 World final. From left to right they are: John Cayzer (381), Bob Perry (217), Doug McMahon (213), Tony May (364), Geoff Goddard (294) and scotsman Vic Russell (94). World Championships were 'all-ticket' events in the early 1970s, attracting huge crowds.

East Anglian driver Jack Savage (255) on the grand parade at Wimbledon. What would today's health and safety executives make of drivers smoking cigarettes on a parade lap?

The front of the grid for the 1970 Superstox World Championship at Wimbledon. A European car has drawn pole position with Pete Welland (264) on the outside.

Geoff Goddard's hopes of winning the 1970 World Championship ended with this roll-over. A bad day for him then, but he was to win the title in 1971 and 1972 before rolling again in 1973 during his attempt to win it for the third time on the trot. Next to Geoff's stricken car is that of Dutchman Berrie van den Oetlelaar.

Ready to roll going into the pit bend at Wimbledon stadium in 1970. The white tops are led by Tony Green (outside, left) and Fred Cracknell (43).

Opposite: Biffo Sweeney celebrates his win in the Superstox World Championship at Wimbledon on 12 September 1970. The World title capped a very good year for Biffo as he also took third place in the British Championship (at Ipswich) and in the European Championship at Cowdenbeath.

Spedeworth's immaculate Ford Capri control car leading an early 1970s Superstox grand parade. The start marshal aboard the back of the car is Alan Butler.

The yellow-graders line up under the lights at Wimbledon stadium in 1970. Nearest the camera is Roger Finch (424). On his outside is John Field (160).

The 1970 visit by the South African team alerted Spedeworth to the potential of team racing. Each stadium was to have its own team in the league with cars specially built for the non-contact races. The concept was called 'Auto Speedway' and this is the prototype car (based loosely on the South African machines) pictured under the floodlights at Aldershot Stadium.

Keith Fransella was one of the Superstox drivers picked to join the Wimbledon Canaries (later known as the Dons) team in the Auto Speedway league. Keith started racing stock cars in 1966 and later moved into Midget racing after the league folded in 1972. He retired from racing in 1977.

Auto Speedway action at Wimbledon stadium. Dons racer Steve Monk (443) leads Hot Rod regular Mick Collard (having a very rare Superstox outing) around Plough Lane.

More action at Wimbledon. The Dons are at home to double-league championship winners, the Wisbech Fen Tigers. Tony May (Tigers) points his 364 car inside Barry Plummer (Dons, 529) while Steve Monk (Dons, 443) leads the trio.

Biffo Sweeney (530) chases Mark Eaton (18) around Ipswich *c.* 1971. Both are racing in Auto Speedway bodied cars although the background shows a more traditional style superstox car, so it is unclear if this is actually a team match. Both cars sport the red, blue and white livery of the 'Cross in Hand Tigers' team.

Hampshire racer John Field (160) and Sussex man Rod Waller (20) competing in Auto Speedway cars at Wimbledon. Field represented the Aldershot Knights while Waller was part of the Eastbourne Lions team. This picture was taken at Wimbledon and therefore is probably a regular Superstox meeting rather than a Speedway fixture.

Popular Felixstowe driver Norman Crowe in action. A still photo of Norman's distinctively striped livery appeared in the opening titles for the children's television programme *Screen Test*.

Steve Monk leads Roy Wood at a wet Aldershot meeting. Wood was a great innovator and is seen here in an unusual low-slung, rear-engine car. This style of car did not catch on.

Surrey garage proprietor and long-time Superstox star Gordon Street leads Steve Monk at Lydden Hill. Safety officials today would wince at the lack of barriers or run-off on the outside of the circuit.

This page and opposite: When Steve Monk did anything on circuit he usually did it well, including this spectacular roll sequence over at Cross in Hand. It's perhaps all too easy to focus on crashes but even champions have off-days. Steve was one of the most successful Superstox drivers of the 1970s and the first to win all four of the major titles. He won the World Championship in 1974, the British Championship in 1975, the European Championship in 1976 and the English in 1978. He also held the silver roof of National Points leader in his career.

An early shot of Dave Pierce lining up in his Fiat Topolino bodied car at Cross in Hand. Also in shot are Denny 'The Undertaker' Pearson (319) and Pete Welland (264).

Head-on confrontation with Dave Pierce in the pits at Cross in Hand. The pit area was easily accessible for the fans. You can see the large crowd, typical for this circuit, in the background.

1970 World Champion Biffo Sweeney poses by his car in the pits at Cross in Hand in 1971. Dave Molyneux's MG Magnette stock car (228) is parked up immediately behind.

Better known as a Stock Car driver Eddie George also spent some time in Superstox (and in the fence). He somehow made it through the 'safety' fence at Cross in Hand raceway. This shot also shows just how narrow (and tricky) the Sussex circuit was.

Above: John Gray racing in the original green, black and white team colours of BP Oils and *Custom Car* magazine in 1971. Woodley's Alan Freebody (295) who was third in the 1968 English Championship is on the outside line.

Left: One of many race wins by Reading racer Tony May, who celebrates on the control car at Wimbledon. Tony was the National Points Champion in 1970 and 1972. Although the World title eluded him he won the 1968 European championship in Amsterdam.

Another of the all-time greats, Dave Pierce, takes to the grand parade at Wimbledon. Pierce was the first driver to win the World title when the formula was renamed 'Superstox' in 1968. He also won the National Points Championship. He remained as Points Champion for most of the 1970s but did not manage to win the World title again until 1980.

Early BP Oils/*Custom Car* magazine team member Roger Warnes at Wimbledon in 1971. Warnes was only with the team for a short while – the 1971 season as teammate to John Gray, Dave Pierce and Tony May. 1971 was a good year for the man from King's Lynn as he finished third in the World Championship.

Roy Eaton taking part in a grand parade at Wimbledon Stadium early in his racing career. The circuit doubled up as a speedway track for many years and the shale often made conditions difficult. Times have changed at Wimbledon as speedway bikes now use their own circuit, which nestles inside the tarmac oval raceway.

Jim Davey (407) is shown the way onto the circuit for an early 1970s grand parade at Wimbledon. Jim was a member of the Wimbledon Dons Auto Speedway team but is pictured here in his own distinctive car rather than one of the team cars.

Gordon Maidment's smart car in action at the 1972 British Superstox Championship meeting at Ipswich. Being a Southampton-domiciled driver, Gordon competed mainly at his local Ringwood raceway.

Opposite, above: German driver Heinz Gobbels steers his Fiat 125 S rear-engine powered superstox around Wimbledon on 30 September 1972 in the World Championship race.

Opposite, below: Steve Monk (443) is challenged by Derry Warwick (40) at Ringwood. Both drivers have successful racing sons. We'll see more of Derry's son, Derek, later in these pages while Steve's son, Derry, became a champion driver in Stock Cars.

Tennant Douglas on the grand parade at Central Park, Cowdenbeath, 3 September 1972. Known as 'The Saint', Tenant was one of the most popular Superstox drivers in Scotland. His successes included the 1969 Scottish Open Championship, where he beat Dave Pierce into second place.

Opposite, above: A win for Scottish ace Bill Crawford at Cowdenbeath late in 1972. Like many second-generation racers Bill's son, Gary, competes on the MSA-controlled circuits in Legends Cars.

Opposite, below: 1972 action at Cowdenbeath. Les Brown (84) swaps ends while Ronnie Nisbet (104) and Malcolm Paterson (107) speed past on the outside. Nisbet won the 1971 Scottish Open.

Above: Racing at Wimbledon stadium on Saturday evenings was all the more atmospheric at night when staged under the floodlights. In a formula where the best drivers have to start at the back of the grid only a few would get this view at the start of a race – the rear end of Tony May's multi-race winning car.

Right: Double Superstox World Champion Geoff Goddard at the British Championship meeting at Ipswich in 1972. Geoff emigrated to South Africa in the early 1970s after a very successful career in Superstox.

An impressive line-up of superstox at Ipswich in 1972. John Gray is using his Wisbech Tigers Auto Speedway team car although he still carries the logos of BP and *Custom Car*. Immediately behind John is Bob Perry with Dave Pierce (320) alongside.

The rolling lap for the start of the 1972 World Superstox Championship at Wimbledon. At this stage the European drivers were still using rear-engine cars as can be seen by the car on the outside of the front row.

Derek Warwick won the 1973 World Superstox Championship at Wimbledon and went on to become the pride of all short oval racing by moving onto the circuits and climbing through the ranks into Grand Prix racing. Although he was a very popular Superstox racer, what really endeared him to the fans over the years was that he never forgot his roots in the sport.

South African champion Bobby Scott splashes through the rain at Wisbech in one of the Test matches against the English team during 1973. Like Derek Warwick, Scott moved onto the RAC-controlled circuits and in fact raced in Formula Ford's 'World Cup' against Warwick in 1976.

Roy Freemantle (419) chased by Norman Hicks (244) at Oxford. The shale circuit only saw action under the Spedeworth banner during the 1973 season and this photo was taken at the opening meeting. Freemantle's car is one of many to sport a roof mascot, in this case a 'Homepride' man!

Two future World Champions line up next to each other – Steve Monk (443) with Neil Bee (482). Behind them is Pete Welland (264) at the former Olympic stadium, White City, in London.

An early picture of long-time racer Brian Jones on the grand parade at a busy Matchams Park, Ringwood. Based in Tadworth, Surrey, Brian was a consistent driver who retained star status for most of his racing career.

Scottish star driver John Duncker (9) chases Steve Monk (443) at Ipswich for the 1973 British Championship. Steve borrowed Bill Bridges' car for this event. Duncker's best international finish was second place in the 1974 Scottish Open.

Tich Jermyn (865) in trouble at Ipswich with Steve Monk (443) and Roy Freemantle (419) also involved. A good crowd shows plenty of support for East Anglian aces Bob Perry (217) and Skid Parrish (69).

The BP Oils/*Custom Car* magazine team launched a new livery in this 1973 photo call at Aldershot stadium. Dave Pierce lines up next to his teammate Tony May. Pierce swapped the Toplino bodied car for one with a team body in the 1974 season.

Opposite, above: Action from an England *v.* South Africa Test match. Geoff Fry (105) leads compatriot Gert Myburgh (27) while English aces Roger Warnes (417) and Rick Drewery (352) give chase. The South Africans bought a strong team of five drivers to contest both the Test series and the individual Superstox World Championship. England won the series 4–2.

Opposite, below: Scottish stars Les Clarke (39, nearest camera) and Bill Cunningham (325) await the draw for the Superstox World Championship at Wimbledon.

Dave Willis moved into Superstox from Stock Cars in 1973 and initially used this ex-Auto Speedway team car bought from Jim Davey. Dave is pictured prior to racing on the shale at the Oxford stadium.

Tony May's immaculate and well-set-up car gets some pre-1973 season practice at Aldershot stadium.

Fire at Cowdenbeath! One of the most horrifying situations on the race track is a car bursting into flames. Fortunately Scottish regular Mike Jack is out of the car.

Alan Cayzer in action at Wimbledon in 1974. Alan was the older of the two Cayzer brothers and had a career that spanned some twenty-seven years from 1964 to 1991 racing BriSCA Formula One Stock Cars as well as Superstox.

Defending champion Derek Warwick awaits the draw for the 1974 World Championship under the floodlights. Behind Derek is Scottish qualifier Bill Crawford (75)

With a full grid of the sport's top drivers in place, the rolling start lap for the 1974 World Championship is underway. Aboard the Ford Cortina control car the well-loved start marshal Ted Weaver ensures that an orderly start ensues.

Opposite, below: Ready for the off in the 1974 World Championship, which was taking place at its traditional home, Plough Lane, Wimbledon. The grid has been drawn by public ballot with Steve Monk (443) drawing pole position. Alongside Steve on the front row is East Anglian driver Doug McMahon. Spedeworth's brand of Stock Car racing featured intense rivalry between Southern-based drivers and those from East Anglia. The Anglian drivers did well in the draw for the 1974 championship with Alan Cayzer (380) third on the grid behind Monk and Stu Blyth (235) on the outside of the second row. Monk, a late reserve entry, went on to win the race.

1974 Superstox action at Cowdenbeath. Dennis Arthur (30) leads Orr Thomson (47) and Malcolm Paterson (107). Paterson was one of the first Scottish drivers to take on and regularly beat the English. He won the 1970 European and 1974 British Championships.

1974 World Champion Derek Warwick (221), on a visit to Cowdenbeath in 1975, is chased by Ian Edmiston.

John Field in action at Wimbledon in 1974. The Headley Down motor engineer was a surprise qualifier for the World Championship but was out of luck in the big race after drawing grid position thirty-two (out of thirty-five).

Norwich-based driver Alan Taylor nearing the end of his Superstox career at Wimbledon in 1974 where he took sixth in the World Championship. He maintained red grade for much of the time he was racing and also represented his home circuit, Great Yarmouth, in Auto Speedway.

Two 'visitors' for the 1974 World Superstox Championship at Wimbledon. Al Contreras (770) was the American representative although he was in fact a regular racer in the UK (being an airman based in East Anglia). Les Clark (39) was one of the top Scottish drivers. Legendary start marshal Ted Weaver (walking between the cars) is about to check that the pair are strapped in and ready for the start.

Opposite, above: Wimbledon stadium always provided some great racing but the main headache for the officials was when conditions were wet and the cars could only be recognised by the fin numbers they carried. When conditions were particularly bad even the roof numbers became covered, leaving the lap scorers to identify the cars by their body shapes.

Opposite, below: A shale-covered super opposite-locking at Wimbledon.

On the grid for the 1974 World final at Wimbledon. Bill Bridges (258) sits on the outside of row six. Directly ahead of him is Bob Perry (217) with Dave Pierce (320) on the inside. Perry and Pierce diced for most of the race with the former crashing on the final bend! Ahead of Perry on the grid is Scotsman Malcolm Paterson who drove well (away from home) to take fourth place.

Stu Blyth (235) and Alan Cayzer (380) ready for the off at Wimbledon. Blyth in particular always had a reputation for racing well-prepared cars.

South African entrant Leon Elza spins out in the 1974 World Championship at Wimbledon. Scotsman Les Clark whizzes past.

Gordon Street was another long-serving driver in Superstox and another to miss out on major title wins. He was never too far away from the top of the points chart, however, and bagged several decent places in trophy races including fourth in the 1974 English Championship.

Richmond-based Alan Oates was around for only a short while although he qualified as a reserve for the 1974 World Championship. He made the grid as a late replacement for the absent Dutchman Ben Mulder and is seen readying the car for the event.

Many of the European drivers due to compete in the 1974 World Superstox Championship did not arrive in time owing to bad weather. The South African team of Leon Elza (nearest camera) and Geoff Fry had their cars shipped to the UK well in advance and easily made it into the field. Fry's car was the only one in the race to use a Peugeot engine

An unusual view of Bert Hawkins' car on it's transporter at Wimbledon. A long-time racer, Bert won the English Superstox Championship at Wimbledon in 1984. He also had spells racing in hot rods and stock rods.

Frenetic action from Ipswich in 1975. Red-graded drivers Roger Finch (424) and Paul Conde (36) are busy passing blue-graded Keith Goodings (354), Bert Hawkins (721) and Brian Jones (685).

Opposite, above: Long-time Superstox pilot Pete Welland takes to the Foxhall speedway circuit in avoidance of a spinner on the back straight. Pete was third in the 1970 World Championship and then second in 1972.

Opposite, below: Typically close Superstox action at Wisbech. BP Oils/*Custom Car* team man John Gray (546) dices with fellow BP Oils-backed Steve Monk (443) and Butch Goodings.

Les Brown (84) sticks the bumper into an unfortunate spinner at Cowdenbeath while Bill Crawford (75) helps him along. Brown took third place in the 1976 Scottish Championship.

Reigate racer Tony Smith-Weller produced this unusual superstox – a Triumph GT6. The theory behind using a 'stock' Triumph was that most superstox at the time used Triumph suspension parts. The car was not a success – an immediate handicap was that it was right-hand drive, putting the driver weight on the outside.

Close racing from the blue tops at the 1975 Spedeweekend. Tony Smith-Weller (in a more conventional car) puts the bumper into Paul Pearson (397), these two making the most of the inside line to get the better of Ron Harrison (61) and Pete Anderson (56).

Two 1975 Superstox drivers better known for racing in other formulae. Bill Bryant (245) later produced a smart hot rod while Paul Conde (36) raced very successfully in the 3-litre Super Rod class in the late 1970s.

Two attractive home-built cars that epitomise Superstox in the mid-1970s. High Wycombe racer Pete Anderson (56) leads Martin Burch (263) around the turnstile bend at Ipswich.

Opposite, above: Jack Savage (255), Pete Anderson (56) and Stu Blyth (235) at Ipswich. Blyth later moved into V8 Stock Cars and has won both the World and European titles.

Opposite, below: Barry Plummer was a star driver for quite a while in the Superstox and most often went best at his home circuit, Wimbledon. Barry also tried his hand at Midget racing in the late 1960s but was better known as a consistently fast red-graded pilot in the 'Supers'. He was also a member of the Wimbledon Dons (Auto Speedway) team.

Dave Willis charges around Wimbledon with the leaderboard telling us that he's on his way to another race win. The other places are out of shot but for the record are Tony Smith-Weller (494), Alan Barrett (497), John Gray (546), Howard White (170) and Tony Roots (174).

It's Eric Brown in car 45 but the 1975 Cowdenbeath low flier with the detached back axle is not identifiable. Eric's son, also called Eric, is a leading F1 Stock Car driver who also raced in Superstox (and F2) earlier in his career.

John Gray in action in 1976. John, from Downham Market in Norfolk, was twice English Champion, winning the title at Wimbledon in 1970 and in 1985 at Wisbech. His best shot at the world title was second place in 1975. He finally retired from racing in 1986.

1975 World Champion Neil Bee at Ipswich. Neil won the title for the first time at Kaldenkirchen in Germany. He went on to win three more World titles, in 1981, 1982 and 1986. After starting racing as a teenager in 1971 Neil rose quickly through the grades, going from white to red grade in just four months. He raced in every season up to and including 1991 when, sadly, he died from cancer aged thirty-six. An annual trophy race is contested in Superstox in Neil's memory.

Opposite above: John Cayzer pictured at Ipswich in 1975, the year he won his first major title, the English Championship (at Wisbech in August). He retained the title in 1976. John later made a successful move into BriSCA Formula One Stox.

Opposite below: Gordon 'Spotty' McDougall pictured in his World Championship-winning season (1976) but before he had won the title. Regular Southern England driver John Fenton (403) is also in shot.

Race action from Ipswich in 1976. Steve Monk (443) leads here from the man who took over the mantle of World Champion in 1975, Neil Bee (482). Chasing them both is Alan Cayzer (380).

Mark Eaton's well-prepared superstox in action at Ipswich in 1976. He eventually became World Champion in 2001 (in the renamed SX2000 Formula) but had a couple of other podium finishes in 'majors' including the 1975 European and a win in the 1976 London Championship.

Jim Kendall's car may have had a boxy look to it but it was good enough to take him to red grade.

Paul Pearson (397) being chased by Colin Bradley (481) at Ipswich in 1976. Maidenhead racer Pearson started to pickup up some useful results in the 1980s and continued to race well into the 1990s.

Roy Eaton retires from the 1976 British Championship race with Howard White (170) going past in the background. The two drivers were both winners of the English Championship at Wimbledon – Eaton in 1973 and White in 1980.

Bob Perry (217) on his way to regaining the British Championship at Ipswich in 1976. He was given a hard time in the race by blue-graded driver Keith 'Butch' Goodings who eventually finished second with Howard White in third. Perry first won the British title in 1973, again at Ipswich.

Butch Goodings and Keith Watson (328) in action during the 1976 British Championship.

Long-time top Scottish driver Vic Russell won the World title in 1985, but that's nine years away here as he lines his car up to pass Southern driver Alan Barrett at Ipswich in 1976.

Opposite, above: Johnny Coupland (24) racing with Colin Bradley (481). Four years after the demise of the Auto Speedway league the team-bodied cars are still in evidence and going strong (in the blue grade). Coupland did not stay with Superstox much longer as he took up Super Rod racing and later became the promoter at Ringwood.

Opposite, below: The World Superstox Championship was traditionally held at Wimbledon, although it moved away for two seasons, in 1975 to Kaldenkirchen, Germany, and then to Cowdenbeath in 1976. The huge crowd got what they wanted – a win for local star Gordon McDougall – but there was also some impressive action as seen here, with Dave Pierce (320) tangling with fellow Southerner Tony Smith-Weller (494) who is stuck on a marker tyre. Vic Russell (94) looks as if he might just have got out of the way.

Jim Welch stunned the establishment by winning the 1977 World Championship at Wimbledon stadium. Regulars were surprised because Welch was a visiting driver representing the Boston circuit and the first non-Spedeworth driver to win the title. He drew grid place twenty-three in the lottery for starting positions and managed to carve his way through the field and lap everybody else apart from the second-place finisher, Alan Cayzer. Welch is pictured here at Wimbledon in the Winternational meeting at the end of the 1977 season.

Jim Davey (407) pips Dave Pierce (320) to a race win at the Winternational meeting at Wimbledon on New Year's Day 1977. Plough Lane track specialist Davey won both races from Pierce on the day so this could be either the heat or the final! The ITV cameraman (just above the 721 and 320 roof numbers) can be seen capturing the event for live broadcast. The third car in the picture, Bert Hawkins, was a lap down but still finished in sixth and eighth places in the two races.

Above and below: The Sweeney brothers made short-lived returns to the Superstox in 1977. Ten years on from his World Championship-winning season, Adrian 'Todd' Sweeney presented this smart Triumph Herald-bodied car. The practice of using cut-down bodies from road cars for the cabs of superstox was starting to die out at this point although you can also see two Mini-based models in the shot – those of Brian Stacey (242) and Alan Barrett (497). Stacey also had a later car that used a cut-down Morris Marina body.

1970 Word Champion Michael 'Biffo' Sweeney made a brief comeback to the sport in 1977. He was soon winning races and up among the red-graded drivers. He also won the Champion of Champions race at this meeting at Wimbledon.

Belgian Champion Jean-Pierre Delannoy in the pits for the 1977 World Championship at Wimbledon. Delannoy drew position thirty-four – last place – in the ballot for starting positions. Just behind Jean-Pierre's car is Anthony van den Oetelaar who was the top European in the race, finishing sixth.

The Ulster team at the 1977 World Championship included Ray Clifford (7) from Larne and Aghadowey's Willie Jones (5).

A smart, low-slung superstox car from Ulsterman Willie Finnegan on his only visit to Wimbledon stadium for the 1977 World Championship. Finnegan proved his worth in international Superstox racing by taking fourth place in his visit to Cowdenbeath for the 1977 British Championship.

Bill Pullar (left) and Les Clark (right) on turn four at Cowdenbeath in 1977. Both drivers were respected and successful drivers in Scotland and both had good results in internationals. Clark was a Spedeworth Scotland driver right from the promotion's first meeting in 1965. He won the British Championship in 1977 and the European in 1984. Pullar, another long-serving driver, won the European in 1978.

Opposite, above: Typical close action at an Arlington bank holiday race meeting. Brian Jones (685) is heading out of shot chased by Todd Sweeney (533) and Dave Willis (665). At the back of the shot are, from left to right, Volvo-powered Colin Bradley, Bill Bridges, Ken Ginger and Allan Harris.

Opposite, below: Howard Cole pictured at Wimbledon in 1977. He was second in the British Championship that year but went one place better to win the Championship, also at Wimbledon, in 1978. That season proved to be one of his most successful years as he was runner-up in the World Championship, third in the English and fourth in the National Points chart. He went on to become one of the sport's leading chassis constructors but sadly he lost his life in an accident at Ipswich. Like the late Neil Bee, Howard is fondly remembered and a memorial race in his name is contested every year.

Some work is needed on Dave Pierce's car after the meeting final at Wimbledon on 22 April 1978. The car had rolled in spectacular fashion but thankfully Dave was uninjured (you can see him grinning in the group of drivers behind the car. Strangely, another roll-over occurred at exactly the same time at the other end of the circuit as Brian Bearman flipped his car. Earlier in the evening Bryan Kensett had done the same in one of the heats.

Opposite, above: Boston regular Ian King was originally a BriSCA Formula Two Stock Car driver but the affiliation between Spedeworth and Three Star promotions in the late 1970s saw him race on the Southern circuits more often.

Opposite, below: Robin Randall (662) was to become a top Superstox pilot but started off in BriSCA Formula Two Stox. He's pictured here in the pits at a Newton Abbot meeting in 1978 parked up alongside Richard 'Paddy' Parker (630).

A nice muddy pit area at Arlington in the August of 1979 (possibly Bank Holiday Monday) proves that you can never rely on the weather in the UK. Roy Eaton and Alan Harris are parked up behind the back-straight grandstand, which is still under construction in the shot.

The idea of licensed drivers racing on non-licensed circuits was very much frowned upon. Alan Hawkins (son of Bert Hawkins, seen earlier in the book) took a day off from racing his superstox with Spedeworth to shake it down on the Layhams Farm grass circuit near New Addington in Surrey in August 1979. Superstox raced officially on grass in 1975 when Spedeworth raced at Billingshurst and Great Chart.

Here's Alan Hawkins where we would expect to see him – in the pits at his home track, Wimbledon.

A view from the back-straight grandstand of the action from a Bank Holiday meeting at Arlington. The large crowd is enjoying some typically close Superstox action, with Dave Pierce moving up on the inside of East Anglian visitor Stu Mensley as the cars enter the back straight.

Bill Bridges drives through the pits at Arlington ready to take in some practice. The three stock cars in the background are Kevin Shinn (Escort), Geoff Morris (591, Cortina) and Rob Sayers (just showing the rear end of his Vauxhall).

Star driver Paul Pearson readies himself for practice at a wet and muddy Aldershot stadium in 1979. Paul bought the car from former World Champion Todd Sweeney.

Above and below: Robin Randall's switch to Superstox followed his racing in F2 specification at an open meeting held at Wimbledon. Randall was the only BriSCA driver to turn up. He ended his first race in the fence and competed in the final without a front bumper, but still scored a respectable placing. He doesn't look too unhappy, though, being pushed back to the pits through the tunnel.

'Down Town' Tadworth-based driver Brian Jones emerges for a race at Arlington in 1979. Jones always produced a neat car. This one stayed true to the 'stock' element of the name and sported a cut-down Datsun body.

Derek Hales in the pit area at Aldershot. The car is one of the first built by Cornish builder Colin Higman to be seen in Superstox. 'Higmans' were, up to this point, more successful in BriSCA Formula Two. These days Hales runs the short oval Legends Cars.

Surrey-based Superstox novices Paul Youngman (20, left of picture) and Mark Norris (257) dicing on the home straight at Aldershot stadium in 1979.

Roy Eaton makes his way from the pit area to the circuit for the grand parade at Arlington. By now the Superstox had a fifth grade in addition to the traditional white, yellow, blue and red. The 'Superstars' were signified by a red, white and blue stripe being sported on the roof.

Other titles published by Tempus

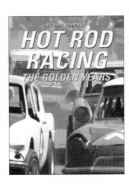

Hot Rod Racing

RICHARD JOHN NEIL

The 1970s saw hot rod racing at the height of its popularity, with large crowds flocking to watch their heroes in action every week. Over the decade the hot rod class moved from being a sport for the working man to one that had professional teams racing in a national Grand Prix series. Captured here in over 200 photographs are the cars, the drivers, the circuits and the events from those golden years of racing.

0 7524 3241 9

Oval Racing in Devon and Cornwall

ANDREW WELTCH

The Thrill of the Century is how promoters labelled stock-car racing, when it arrived in the South-West of England in 1954. The spectacle of motor racing on short oval tracks was an instant hit, and drivers from Devon and Cornwall were among the first stars of the sport. This book includes photographs of stock cars, hot rods, midgets, bangers and other classes that have raced on the tracks in St Austell, St Day and St Columb in Cornwall, and at Plymouth, Exeter, Newton Abbot and Smeatharpe in Devon over the last fifty years.

0 7524 2931 0

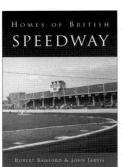

Homes of British Speedway

ROBERT BAMFORD & JOHN JARVIS

This book features over 300 venues. Every track is afforded statistical information, a synopsis and illustrations. Compiled by Robert Bamford, a prolific author of speedway titles, and John Jarvis, a leading historian and enthusiast of the sport in the modern era, this book is an essential purchase for anyone with an interest in the shale sport. An ambitious and comprehensive work, it is the definitive history and guide to the homes of British speedway.

0 7524 2210 3

Speedway through the Lens of Mike Patrick

MIKE PATRICK

A familiar figure to anyone who is interested in speedway, Mike Patrick tirelessly (and often bravely) goes further than any other photographer in the field to get the most original and impressive shots. This is a selection of his finest images; famous riders at work and play, amazing action shots, and important moments make this an essential edition to the collection of any speedway fan.

0 7524 2596 X

If you are interested in purchasing other books published by Tempus, or in case you have difficulty finding any Tempus books in your local bookshop, you can also place orders directly through our website

www.tempus-publishing.com